"much love, Mom
7-6-18

Katherine Dunn

big !
*

I Wish

A GOOD BOOK FOR PONDERING

by Katherine Marris

Published by Willis Harding, LLC
227 Sandy Springs Circle, Suite D-197
Sandy Springs, GA 30328

Printed in China

I Wish, A Good Book for Pondering / Katherine Marris.

FIRST EDITION, 2009

ISBN-10: 0-615-28240-7
ISBN-13: 978-0-615-28240-4

Who knew I would be granted
three perfect wishes
Cameron, Nick and Piper Kate

Acknowledgements

When you have misplaced your Jiminy, you don't want to go on the hunt alone. And I didn't.

Thanks Guys —

God gives us gifts and talents to nurture and use and I am thankful to Him.

Brooke French, the most devoted and fine friend a person could wish for;

Cameron Cashion, the first to see my vision for this book and said "go for it, Mom", who I adore and listen to when she twirls her hair as she gives me her opinion of what young adults think and feel;

Nick Thomas, my level-headed pragmatist who tells the truth at all times, whether you want to hear it or not, you keep me honest;

Ashley Miller aka "boo boo" – I'm proud to be your nusky Mom;

Madelyn Mansfield, an artist with immaculate taste;

Melody Baker (that's Melody like the song, Baker – one k) who is not really arrogant at all;

Pamela Jacobson, the empress of design layout patience;

my best friends and rock Christina and Terry Adams, the kind of friends only God can give you;

Nancy Jane, sister extraordinaire;

and of course Pip Pip who is not only a wish, but a dream come true!

$\mathcal{A}$ prayer in its simplest definition
is merely a wish turned Godward.
Phillips Brooks

$\mathcal{S}$top the habit of wishful thinking and start the habit of thoughtful wishes.
Mary Martin

$\mathcal{P}$ray till prayer makes you forget your own wish,
and leave it or merge it in God's will.
Frederick William Robertson

When you wish upon a star,
makes no difference who you are.

When you wish upon a star,
your dreams come true.

– Jiminy Cricket

I wish...

Mornings
didn't start
so early

and I wish...

Double chins were all the rage

I wish...

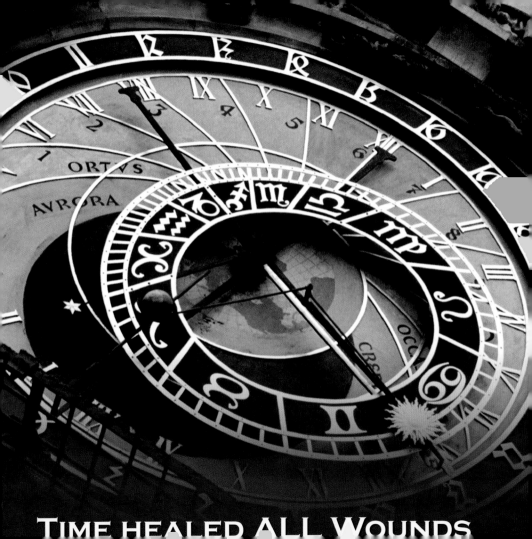

TIME HEALED ALL WOUNDS

I really wish...

Crystal and feelings

weren't so fragile

And

A smile was  mandatory

and I wish...

Wisdom and Truth were more valued than Status and Position

And

I could fly on a trapeze just once

I really wish...

Dogs lived as long as people

I wish...

The Waltz was still popular

and I wish...

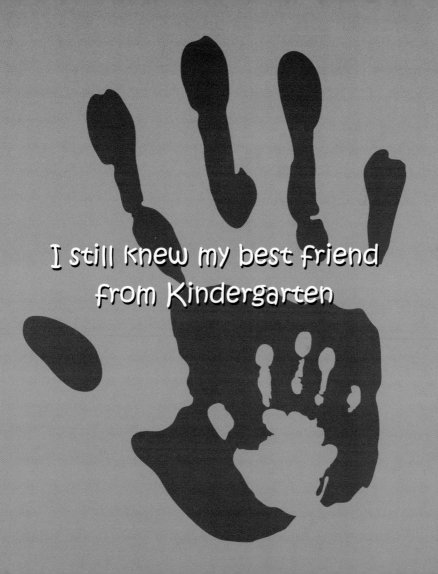

I still knew my best friend
from Kindergarten

And

Knees lasted a lifetime

I wish...

There was a fifth season called...

Linger

I really wish...

We were more proud of our tears

I wish...

I could hear angel wings

I really wish...

Everyone could go home

and I wish...

I had the imagination of a four year old

And

Manicures
weren't fashionable

I wish...

My Mom could read me
a bedtime story

and I wish...

44

TAXES WERE
VOLUNTARY
AFTER 50

I wish...

I really wish...

I was more Merciful

And

Age spots were beauty marks

I wish...

*Success wasn't measured,
but celebrated!*

I really wish...

Everyone could see the
Ocean at least once

I wish...

and I wish...

I had dyed my hair pink just once

And

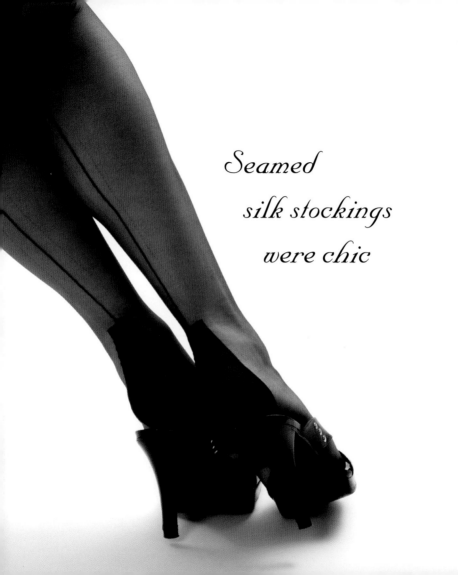

Seamed

silk stockings

were chic

I really wish...

Right: Juliet's house in Verona, Italy,
where lover's leave messages

and I wish...

We could grasp the concept
that happiness

is a by-product of peace

I really wish...

My bed linens
smelled like
sunshine

And

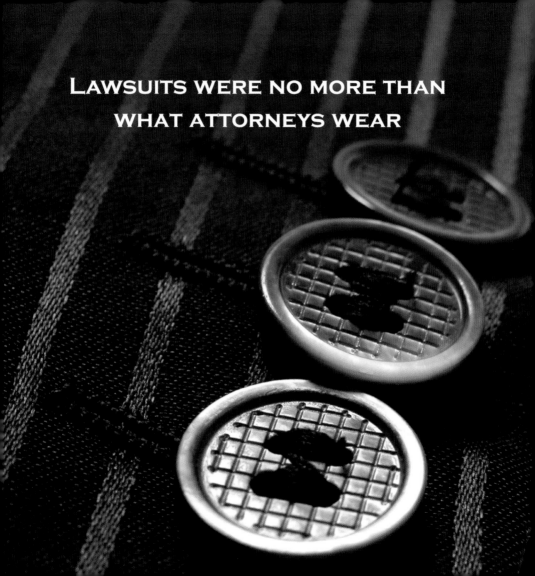

LAWSUITS WERE NO MORE THAN
WHAT ATTORNEYS WEAR

I wish...

Gray Hair
Was Enviable

I wish...

I COULD GET
INTO A MAN'S HEAD
FOR 10 MINUTES

(I don't think I'd want to stay any longer)

and I wish...

i HAD a
TReE HOUSE

I really wish...

WE ALL HAD THE FAITH
OF A MUSTARD SEED

And

Good judgment was
more esteemed than beauty

I wish...

Hotel pillows were always new

and I wish...

My kids knew how much
I love them

I wish...

I knew what to say at funerals

I really wish...

I was long legged,
lean and loved beets
and brussel sprouts

And

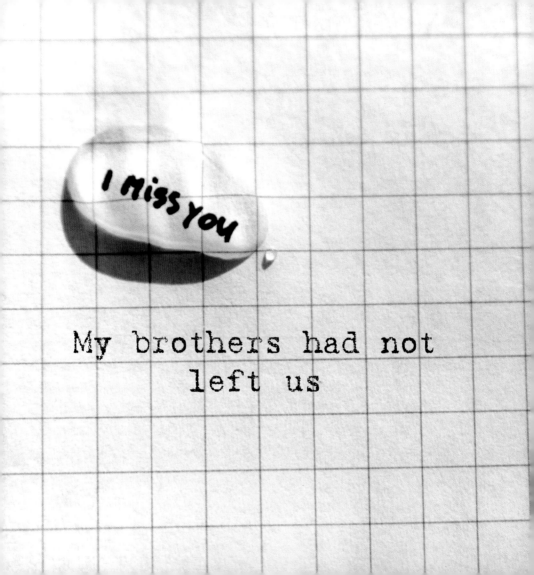

I miss you

My brothers had not
left us

I wish...

We looked for knowledge in all the right places

and I wish...

The best part of
our makeup wasn't
on our face

I wish...

Muffin tops only came out of my oven

I really wish...

I could go to my Grandma's
for one more
Fried Chicken dinner

I wish...

And

I could slide down a Rainbow

I really wish...

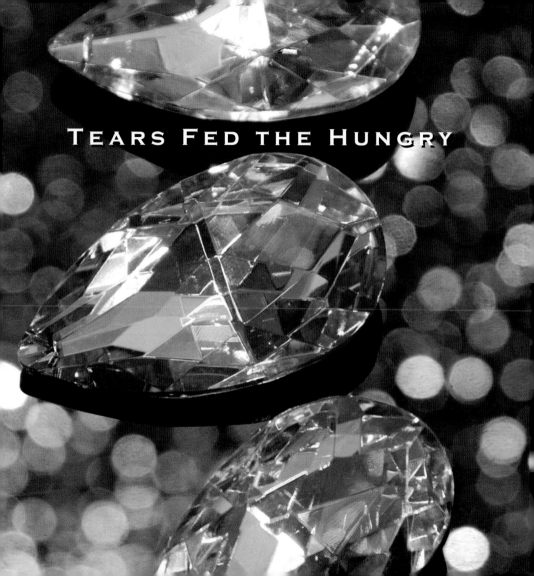

TEARS FED THE HUNGRY

I wish...

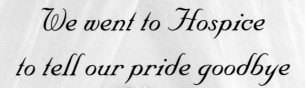

We went to Hospice
to tell our pride goodbye

and I wish...

And

It didn't look ridiculous
when I skip

I wish...

Everyone knew

God's love

I really wish...

I could fly
for one day

I wish...

114

Everyone had parents
as wonderful as I did

I wish...

HUMILITY

WAS
CONTAGIOUS

and I wish...

I made more time to watch clouds

And

Chocolate didn't taste good

(well, maybe not)

I really wish...

For you to live true to your wishes
from this day forward...

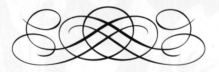

I wish thy way. And when in me myself should rise,
and long for something otherwise,
Then Lord, take sword and spear And slay.
Amy Carmichael

*N*o matter how happily a woman may be married, it always pleases her to discover
that there is a really nice man who wishes she were not.
Mary Catherine Bateson